Digging My Way Out

An In-depth Study of the Word of God

Student Edition

Byron Holloway

Digging My Way Out Student Edition

Copyright © 2017 Byron Holloway

Cover design by RLSimith Designs

Editing and formatting by

Destiny House Publishing, LLC

www.destinyhousepublishing.com

inquiry@destinyhousepublishing.com

P.O. Box 19774

Detroit, MI 48219

All rights reserved.

ISBN-10: 1936867311

ISBN-13: 978-1-936867-31-8

BYRON HOLLOWAY

DEDICATION

I dedicate this book to my loving wife of 12 years Evangelist Gwendolyn Holloway for standing by my side while I spent time praying, studying, researching and writing this book and my Living Bread Ministry family who have shown great support as I embark on this new chapter in my life.

CONTENTS

	Acknowledgments	Pg. 8
1	Introduction	Pg. 9
2	How Do We Know the Bible Is True?	Pg. 12
3	Break Down of Bible & Dates	Pg. 20
4	Rule of Interpretation	Pg. 30
5	S.O.A.P. /Homiletics & Hermeneutics	Pg. 66
6	Exegesis & Eisegesis plus Worksheet	Pg. 75
7	Evangelism	Pg. 89
	About the Author	Pg. 98

ACKNOWLEDGMENTS

I want to acknowledge Apostle Oscar & Prophets Crystal Jones who are very instrumental in me starting and completing my first of many projects. They have inspired me and have given me the necessary tools that I needed to accomplish this task. I also want to give thanks to Pastor Cornelius Bracy for motivating me to dig deep for the Biblical truths that are in the Word of God.

CHAPTER ONE
INTRODUCTION

I was led by the spirit to write this instructional manual for students of the Word who want to go to the next level in their understanding of the Scriptures. This manual will help them understand context is king, correct interpretation, exegesis & eisegesis, homiletics and hermeneutics.

This manual has homework assignments and a preachers work sheet to help students build sermons.

Syllabus Content

Syllabus Statement

Hebrews 5:12-14
[12] For when for the time ye ought to be teachers, ye have need that one teach you again which be the first principles of the oracles of God; and are become such as have need of milk, and not of strong meat. [13] For every one that useth milk is unskillful in the word of righteousness: for he is a babe. [14] But strong meat belongeth to them that are of full age, even those who by reason of use have their senses exercised to discern both good and evil.

Hebrews 6: 1 Therefore leaving the principles of the doctrine of Christ, let us go on unto perfection; not laying again the foundation of <u>repentance from dead works, and of faith toward God, **2** Of the doctrine of baptisms, and of laying on of hands, and of resurrection of the dead, and of eternal judgment.</u>

Course Description

This course examines the validity of the Bible, interpretation, Homiletics & Hermeneutics, expository preaching, the dating of each book and the exegesis & eisegesis of text. Each student at the end of this course is expected to be able to write and articulate a sermon using the course material as a guide. The course is approximately 5 to 6 months.

Course Objectives

How do we know that the Bible is true: Prove that the Bible is the written word of God.
Break down of the Bible & dates: Categorize the books
Rules of Interpretation: learn how to correctly interpret the Bible
Homiletics & hermeneutics: learn the art of preaching, sermon preparation, the importance of context and the correct approach to the text.
Preacher's exegesis worksheet: complete the worksheet (preselected topics)
Evangelism: Learn what is expected of believers.

Course Guidelines

All students are expected to attend all classes unless an exception has been made before the start of the course. Students are required to complete all homework assignments before the start of the next class, unless the instructor informs you otherwise.

It is the responsibility of each student to do the research and to obtain a study partner, if needed.

HOMEWORK ASSIGNMENTS

1. **How do we know that the Bible is true?** Write a 1,000-word essay proving that the Bible is the written word of God. Due Date:
2. **River of Inspiration**
   Write a short overview of each book explaining its reason for being in the Bible, and verify dates.
   Due Date:

3. **Rules of Interpretation** (Examining quotations in the light of both context)

   Give an example of this and its meaning, quote Old and New Testament text.
   Due Date:

4. **S.O.A.P   Scripture, Observation, Application, Prayer**
   What is the meaning of the text? (Exegesis) Essay on Matthew 19:24
   Due Date:

5. **Preacher's exegesis work sheet**
   Complete work sheet (Topics to be given by instructor)
   Due Date:

6. **Evangelism**
   Write a 1000-word essay on the steps of evangelism as it relates to St John 4:1-42
   Due Date:

CHAPTER TWO
HOW DO WE KNOW THE BIBLE IS TRUE?

There have been hundreds of books written on the subject of the evidences of the divine inspiration of the Bible, and these evidences are many and varied. Most people today, unfortunately, have not read any of these books. In fact, few have even read the Bible itself! Thus, many people tend to go along with the popular delusion that the Bible is full of mistakes and is no longer relevant to our modern world.

Nevertheless, the Bible writers claimed repeatedly that they were transmitting the very Word of God, infallible and authoritative in the highest degree. This is an amazing thing for any writer to say, and if the forty or so men who wrote the Scriptures were wrong in these claims, then they must have been lying, or insane, or both.

But, on the other hand, if the greatest and most influential book of the ages, containing the most beautiful literature and the most perfect moral code ever devised, was written by deceiving fanatics, then what hope is there for us ever finding meaning and purpose in this world?

If one will seriously investigate these biblical evidences, he will find that their claims of divine inspiration (stated over 3,000 times, in various ways) were amply justified.

Fulfilled Prophecies

The remarkable evidence of fulfilled prophecy is just one case in point. Hundreds of Bible prophecies have been fulfilled, often long after the prophetic writer had passed away.

For example, Daniel the prophet predicted in about 538 BC (Daniel 9:24-27) that Christ would come as Israel's promised Savior and Prince 483 years after the Persian emperor would give the Jews authority to rebuild Jerusalem, which was then in ruins. This was clearly and definitely fulfilled, hundreds of years later. There are extensive prophecies dealing with individual nations and cities and with the course of history in general, all of which have been literally fulfilled. More than 300 prophecies were fulfilled by Christ Himself at His first coming. Other prophecies deal with the spread of Christianity, as well as various false religions, and many other subjects. Only the Bible manifests this remarkable prophetic evidence, and it does so on such a tremendous scale as to render completely absurd any explanation other than divine revelation.

Unique Historical Accuracy

The historical accuracy of the Scriptures is likewise in a class by itself, far superior to the written records of Egypt, Assyria, and other early nations. Archeological confirmations of the Biblical record have been almost innumerable in the last century. Dr. Nelson Glueck, probably the greatest modern authority on Israeli archeology, has said:

"No archeological discovery has ever controverted a biblical reference. Scores of archeological findings have been made which confirm in clear outline or in exact detail historical statements in the Bible. And, by the same token, proper evaluation of Biblical *descriptions has often led to amazing discoveries."*

Scientific Accuracy

Another striking evidence of divine inspiration is found in the fact that many of the principles of modern science were recorded as facts of nature in the Bible long before scientists confirmed them experimentally. A sampling of these would include:

- Roundness of the earth
  _____
- Hydrologic cycle
  _____
- Vast number of stars
  _____
- Paramount importance of blood in life processes_____
- Atmospheric circulation
  _____
- Gravitational field
  _____

These are not stated in the technical jargon of modern science, of course, but in terms of the basic world of man's everyday experience; nevertheless, they are completely in accord with the most modern scientific facts.

It is significant also that no real mistake has ever been demonstrated in the Bible—in science, in history, or in any other subject. Many have been claimed, of course, but conservative Bible scholars have always been able to work out reasonable solutions to all such problems.

Unique Structure

The remarkable structure of the Bible should also be stressed. Although it is a collection of 66 books, written by 40 or more different men over a period of 2,000 years, it is clearly one Book, with perfect unity and consistency throughout.

The individual writers, at the time of writing, had no idea that their message was eventually to be incorporated into such a Book, but each nevertheless fits perfectly into place and serves its own unique purpose as a component of the whole. Anyone who diligently studies the Bible will continually find remarkable structural and mathematical patterns woven throughout its fabric, with an intricacy and symmetry incapable of explanation by chance or collusion.

The one consistent theme of the Bible, developing in grandeur from Genesis to Revelation, is God's great work in the <u>creation</u> and <u>redemption</u> of all things, through His only Son, the Lord <u>Jesus Christ</u>.

NOTES

DIGGING MY WAY OUT Student Edition

… BYRON HOLLOWAY

CHAPTER THREE

BREAK DOWN OF BIBLE & DATES

The chart and sidebar of the Old and New Testaments are listed on the following page.

DIGGING MY WAY OUT Student Edition

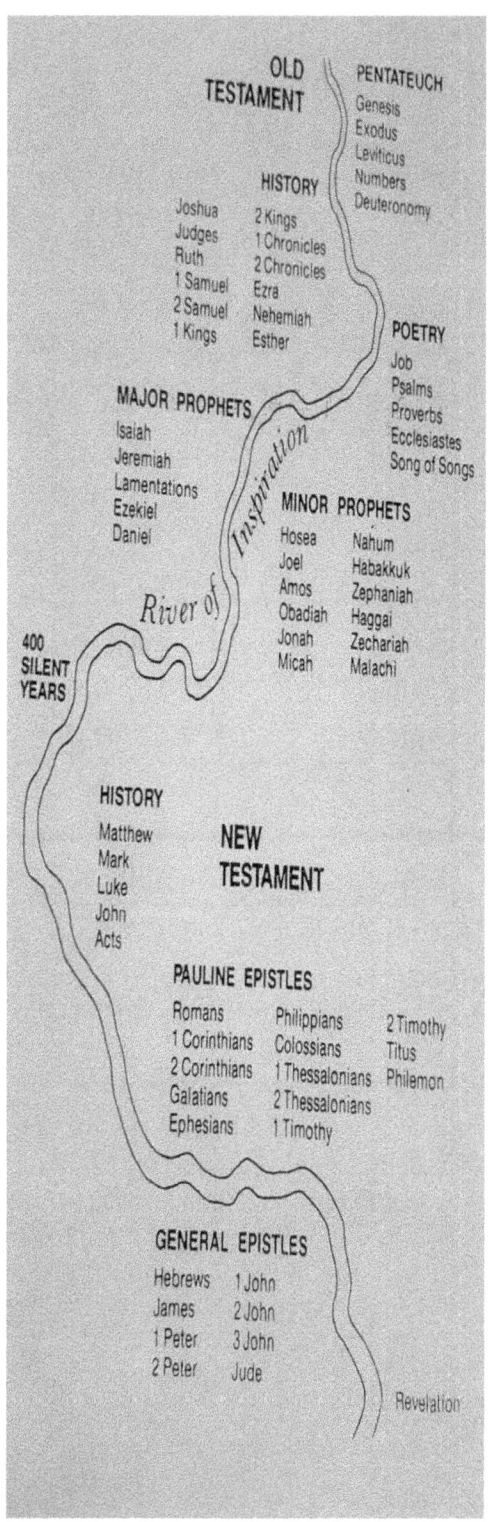

Old Testament

Book	Author	Date Written
Genesis	Moses	?-1445 B.C.
Exodus	Moses	1445-1405 B.C.
Leviticus	Moses	1405 B.C.
Numbers	Moses	1444-1405 B.C.
Deuteronomy	Moses	1405 B.C.
Joshua	Joshua	1404-1390 B.C.
Judges	Samuel	1374-1129 B.C.
Ruth	Samuel	1150? B.C.
First Samuel	Samuel	1043-1011 B.C.
Second Samuel	Ezra?	1011-1004 B.C.
First Kings	Jeremiah?	971-852 B.C.
Second Kings	Jeremiah?	852-587 B.C.
First Chronicles	Ezra?	450-425 B.C.
Second Chronicles	Ezra?	450-425 B.C.
Ezra	Ezra	538-520 B.C.
Nehemiah	Nehemiah	445-425 B.C.
Esther	Mordecai?	465 B.C.
Job	Job?	??
Psalms	David	1000? B.C.
	Sons of Korah wrote Psalms 42, 44-49, 84-85, 87. Asaph wrote Psalms 50, 73-83. Heman wrote Psalm 88. Ethan wrote Psalm 89. Hezekiah wrote Psalms 120-123, 128-130, 132, 134-136. Solomon wrote Psalms 72, 127.	
Proverbs	Solomon wrote 1-29 Agur wrote 30	950-700 B.C.

	Lemuel wrote 31	
Ecclesiastes	Solomon	935 B.C.
Song of Solomon	Solomon	965 B.C.
Isaiah	Isaiah	740-680 B.C.
Jeremiah	Jeremiah	627-585 B.C.
Lamentations	Jeremiah	586 B.C.
Ezekiel	Ezekiel	593-560 B.C.
Daniel	Daniel	605-536 B.C.
Hosea	Hosea	710 B.C.
Joel	Joel	835 B.C.
Amos	Amos	755 B.C.
Obadiah	Obadiah	840 or 586 B.C.
Jonah	Jonah	760 B.C.
Micah	Micah	700 B.C.
Nahum	Nahum	663-612 B.C.
Habakkuk	Habakkuk	607 B.C.
Zephaniah	Zephaniah	625 B.C.
Haggai	Haggai	520 B.C.
Zechariah	Zechariah	520-518 B.C.
Malachi	Malachi	450-600 B.C.

New Testament

Book	Author	Date Written (A.D)
Matthew	Matthew	60's
Mark	John Mark	late 50's early 60's
Luke	Luke	60
John	John	late 80's early 90's
Acts	Luke	61
Romans	Paul	55
1 Corinthians	Paul	54
2 Corinthians	Paul	55
Galatians	Paul	49
Ephesians	Paul	60
Philippians	Paul	61
Colossians	Paul	60
1 Thessalonians	Paul	50-51
2 Thessalonians	Paul	50-51
1 Timothy	Paul	62
2 Timothy	Paul	63
Titus	Paul	62
Philemon	Paul	60
Hebrews	(Paul, Apollos, Barnabas . . . ?)	60's
James	James, half-brother of Jesus	40's or 50's
1 Peter	Peter	63
2 Peter	Peter	63-64
1 John	John	late 80's early 90's

2 John	John	late 80's early 90's
3 John	John	late 80's early 90's
Jude	Jude, half-brother of Jesus	60's or 70's
Revelation	John	late 80's early 90's

Notes

BYRON HOLLOWAY

CHAPTER FOUR
RULES OF INTERPRETATION

THE GOLDEN RULE OF INTERPRETATION

Since the Scriptures are God-breathed and are very specific, there is only one way for us to arrive at the purpose which the Holy Spirit had in mind in giving His message. God said what He meant and He meant exactly what He said. In order to understand the Scriptures, we must know the use of language: the grammar, the specific meaning of words, and the fundamental laws of speech--especially the principles which are characteristic of the Scriptures. Since the space is limited for this discussion, let us look only at the most important and fundamental rules of hermeneutics, the most basic — and indeed the all-inclusive one — of which is the Golden Rule of Interpretation.

Jesus gave the Golden Rule of conduct which is "All things therefore whatsoever ye would that men should do unto you, even so do ye also unto them: for this is the law and the prophets" (Matt. 7:12). This is a basic criterion in one's relation to his fellow-men. The Golden Rule of Interpretation is just as fundamental in the field of the interpretation of language as our Lord's precept is in the realm of ethics and conduct.

Origen, a great Christian scholar who lived during the latter part of the second and the first part of the third century of the Christian Era, came under the influence of Greek philosophy in the form of Neoplatonism (a philosophical system). He adopted some of the so-called principles of this philosophic system and evolved what has become known as the allegorical method of interpreting the Scriptures. According to this theory there is a spiritual meaning of the Bible in addition to that which is plain and obvious. Origen accepted the literal interpretation of the Word, but claimed that in addition to it there was this hidden, spiritual meaning. Everything to him was therefore allegorical. He read into the Scriptures this so-called spiritual meaning and built up a mystical system of theology. This method of interpreting the Word wrought havoc in the early church and started what is known as "spiritualizing the Scriptures." Its destructive effects have been felt throughout the centuries. The Christian world has never entirely freed itself from the tentacles of this heathen, subjective approach to God's holy, infallible Word.

The only antidote to this vicious method of handling the Bible is the principle called the Golden Rule of Interpretation: <u>When the plain, obvious sense of Scripture makes common sense we are to seek no other sense</u>. We are to stop there and are not to read subjectively into the record, something that is foreign to the context. The Word of God is spiritual and does not need our "doctoring" it in order to make it more so. If one man can read into a given context his own ideas and claim that such is the significance of the passage, another can do the same thing and can read into the record his conception of its meaning. Whenever we adopt the spiritualizing method, we open the floodgates to every type of speculation, suggestion, and theorizing. We must not therefore go beyond the plain, literal meaning of the Scriptures unless the facts of the context indicate a deeper, hidden, or symbolic meaning. When therefore such evidence is lacking, one must positively accept the literal meaning of the text.

On the other hand, if there is absolute proof that the language is, for instance, symbolic, then we are to interpret the given passage in the light of all the evidence, not only of the immediate connection, but in the light of that which is found in parallel cases — if there be such.

But suppose the plain, literal meaning does not make common

sense. In that event, we may be assured that since the Scriptures do not make nonsense, a figurative or metaphorical sense is intended. Then we are to interpret such a passage in the light of the usage found in parallel cases.

Almost every word in all languages has not only a literal, primary, original meaning but has derived connotations. For instance, in English there are listed as high as twenty-six meanings for a single word. This fact may be seen by a glance at an unabridged dictionary. Whenever the literal sense of a given word does not fit in with the facts of the connection, we are to select that definition which is in perfect accord and agreement with them. But in every instance, let me emphasize, we are to take the primary, ordinary, usual, literal meaning, if possible.

An abridged statement of this most important rule is: "When the plain sense of Scripture makes common sense, seek no other sense; therefore, take every word at its primary, ordinary, usual literal meaning, unless the facts of the context indicate clearly otherwise." This rule assumes that all truth harmonizes and that there are no discrepancies between accurate statements of facts. But for those who would like a brief expression of a general truth, I give it in the following words.

"**When the plain sense of Scripture makes common sense, seek no other sense**; therefore take every word at its primary, ordinary, usual, literal meaning, unless the facts of the immediate context, studied in the light of related passages and fundamental truths, indicate clearly otherwise." If anyone follows this criteria, in the spirit and letter of the principle, he can never go wrong. On the other hand, if he fails to follow it, he can never be right. (May I suggest that the reader memorize and master this rule in order that he may be governed thereby in all his study of the Word?) This principle is true, not only as it applies to the Bible, but also to any written document or oral conversation regarding any subject.

LAW OF FIRST MENTION

"The law of first mention" is another most important principle involved in the Scriptures. What is meant by it is that the first mention of any fundamental word usually presents the general conception of the subject and its use throughout Scriptures.

As an illustration of this law, I need only to call attention to the sacrifices that were required by the Lord from Cain and Abel. The very fundamental teaching concerning atonement for sin, with all its implications, is found in these sacrifices, as recorded in Genesis 4. Once more, the promise and the covenant which God made with Abraham (Gen. 12:1-3) constitute the bold outline of all that is involved in the divine plan which runs through the Scriptures. It becomes therefore of paramount importance that one study words, doctrines in their original, initial mention in Scripture.

INTERPRETATION AND APPLICATION

As we have just seen in our study of the Golden Rule of Interpretation, we must seek diligently, by the application of this standard, to ascertain the exact thought of the speaker or writer whose message is studied. When this is learned, we can determine whether or not there is involved in the discussion some fundamental principle. If there is such set forth in the given case, we are at liberty to apply it to a similar situation; but, before we do, we must be certain that there is an analogy justifying such an application. It is at this crucial point that many mistakes are made. All too often efforts are made to see a spiritual lesson in a given scripture and, without due consideration, to apply it to another case which only apparently is analogous.

If we are certain that we have discovered the fundamental, underlying principle in a given case, we are warranted in applying it to a like situation under similar circumstances; for one of the basic tenets of true science is that "like causes under like conditions produce like results." My caution to everyone is that he be certain to discover the exact thought of the writer and that he be absolutely sure in making an application of the principle discovered to a similar situation. Such a procedure is legitimate and proper.

LAW OF DOUBLE REFERENCE

There is what is known among Bible students as "the law of double reference or manifold fulfillment of prophecy." We find many applications of this principle.

The prophets constantly spoke of a local or current event, and, without giving any indication of a change of scenery, began to describe a more remote and a greater one, which by far transcended the situation which gave rise to the prediction. This principle might be illustrated by a stereopticon which gives the dissolving effect. One picture is thrown upon the screen. Presently it begins to fade and at the same time the dim outline of another begins to appear. By the time the first has faded, the second is in full view. The prophets often blended a prediction relating to the first coming of Christ with one foretelling the Second Advent. In such presentations the entire Christian Dispensation is passed over. i.e. **Isaiah 9:1-6**

One must master this rule if one is to understand the messages of the prophets.

THE LAW OF RECURRENCE

A principle which obtains throughout the prophetic word is that which is known by Bible students as "the law of recurrence." According to the meaning of this phrase, after the prophets made a statement relative to something in the future, they often gave a fuller discussion covering the same ground but laying the emphasis in a different place. The second presentation is but supplemental to the first. It therefore clarifies the picture.

As an illustration of this principle, may I note **Genesis 1 and 2**? In chapter 1 we have a synopsis of the work of the six days of reconstruction. In chapter 2, however, the Holy Spirit gives a second discussion, especially regarding the creation of man. The first account relative to this miracle is found in **1: 26-31**. In **2: 7-25** is a second and a fuller description together with a record of his residence in the Garden of Eden. These two accounts are not to be explained upon the basis advanced by the destructive critics — that they came from two sources and are therefore contradictory — but upon the sound, fundamental principle of the law of recurrence.

Another illustration of this important law is found in the prophecy of **Ezekiel 38 and 39**, which foretells the invasion of Palestine by the nations constituting the great northeastern confederacy. (For the full discussion of this most important and timely theme, see the volume When Gog's Armies Meet the Almighty.) In chapter **38** the prophet gives the full description of this stupendous world-changing event. In it he presents the general outline of the incidents that will at that time take place. In chapter **39** he simply covers the same ground speaking of the identical affairs but laying emphasis on different things. One must recognize that this duplicate account, given according to the principle of the law of recurrence, is but a second view of the one prediction.

John, in **Revelation 17, 18, and 19**, follows this same law. In chapter **16** he gives the outline of events as they occur during the second half of the Tribulation. When we reach the end of chapter 16, we are at the very close of that period; but in chapter **17** he goes back to the beginning of this second half of it and speaks of the overthrow of Babylon the harlot. The facts of this chapter show that this interpretation is correct. Chapter **18** speaks of the literal city of Babylon, which is destroyed at the end of the Tribulation. In chapter **19** we read of the marriage supper of the Lamb and Christ's coming all the way to earth at the conclusion of the Tribulation. Thus, when John pens these three chapters, after having given the outline of the second half of the Tribulation in chapter 16, he is simply following the law of recurrence.

This is a most important law, which finds many applications throughout the Scriptures. The Bible student should master this principle to the extent that he can recognize an application of it whenever he comes across it.

COMPARING SCRIPTURE WITH SCRIPTURE

God gave His Word as He wanted us to have it, and as He wanted us to study and teach it. An investigation of the Scriptures shows that He only gave a portion of it as there was a demand for the enunciation of some new principle or the reiteration and the augmentation of one that He had already revealed. A study of the life of our Lord shows that He often repeated Himself. We are told that circumstances alter cases. After all, people's experiences are more or less of a certain definite type. These and other facts show why it was necessary for God to repeat certain doctrines in sending messages to various people or groups of individuals. The biblical writers, meeting a local and a similar situation, were forced to repeat many things.

For instance, almost all the books of the New Testament either discuss, refer to, or at least hint at, the great fundamental teaching of regeneration of the soul by the Spirit of God. It was necessary for each writer in meeting the situation before him to refer to this fundamental spiritual phenomenon. To one person or group it was necessary to discuss a certain phase of the doctrine; to another the same writer presented a different aspect of the same teaching. On one occasion, he stated it more fully than he did at another time. What is true of regeneration is also correct of the various teachings of the Word of God.

In view of these facts, we can see how it was that the inspired writers discussed the same subject. If a person is wishing to understand thoroughly any one topic of the Scriptures, it becomes necessary for him to study what each writer has said on the subject. He must, as far as it is possible, get all the facts which called forth the explanation. Moreover he must study it in the light of the facts of its context. When he has thus examined the various passages bearing upon a given question and has gleaned from each reference what is said, he can put all the information together and thus have a complete picture. It is therefore necessary for everyone to compare Scripture with Scripture. In following this principle, he must be absolutely certain that he views each passage in its proper perspective. When he does so, he will see that one account usually supplements another.

STUDY QUOTATIONS IN THE LIGHT OF BOTH CONTEXTS

In the New Testament we see many quotations taken from the Old. Whenever we find in the New Testament such a quotation — if we are not familiar with the passage — we should immediately turn to the chapter from which it was taken. Then we should study the entire connection and be certain that we get the drift of thought of the original writer. Speaking figuratively, we must see the quotation in the original setting. When we have done this, we are to study the context of the New Testament in which this quotation is found. Frequently the application will throw light upon the passage in its original connection and vice versa.

Often we observe that a passage is applied in a certain way to something in the New Testament; and, when we examine all the facts, we see that the thing to which it is referred by the New Testament writer does not fill out the complete picture set forth in the Old Testament connection. In this event, we must conclude that the thing to which it is applied in the New Testament is but a partial and an incomplete fulfillment of the original prediction and that God in His own good time will fulfill the passage to the very letter.

As an illustration of this principle, I may call attention to such passages as **Isaiah 13 and 14** and **Jeremiah 50 and 51**. These chapters give predictions concerning Babylon and its being destroyed. When we look at the history of that city, we see that it was never overthrown in the manner or to the extent as set forth in these prophecies. We do know from ancient history that it gradually declined in power and finally sank beneath the historical horizon. It was never destroyed as was foretold. We who believe the Word of God must conclude that Babylon will yet be rebuilt and demolished just as foretold by these men of God. This is confirmed by **Revelation 18**. I could give numerous examples of this principle, but these suffice. Let us therefore be careful in studying quotations that we examine both contexts and arrive at the definite, specific idea of the inspired writer.

HEBREW POETRY

Thought-rhyme was the fundamental idea of Hebrew poetry. No effort was made at meter, verse, and rhyme as we have in modern poetry. What is Hebrew parallelism? The answer is this: an agreement between two statements that is made relative to a given matter, one of which is made by the selection of certain words. This or a similar idea is repeated by the choice of different terms. The second, therefore, is supplemental to the first and becomes a comment upon it. Sometimes one of the statements is in literal language, whereas the other is more pictorial and, graphic; but each supplements the other. See **Psalms 96: 1-13 & Psalms 98: 1-9**

Upon this simple basis all Hebrew poetry was built. Contrasts were expressed as we see in the Book of Proverbs, which is pure poetry. Frequently three parallel statements, each supplementing the others, were employed. These fundamental conceptions were worked out by the poets and came to involve an entire composition such as one of the Psalms. One must however understand this fundamental conception in order to comprehend the poetical books of the Scriptures.

SYMBOLIC LANGUAGE

All peoples, both ancient and modern, have symbols. The Hebrews had theirs. Those appearing in the Scriptures however are of divine origin. In fact, the Tabernacle and the Temple, with all of their ceremonial services, were typical or symbolic of the realities which we have in Christ. That they had such a significance is set forth clearly in the New Testament. The Book of Hebrews especially interprets the spiritual significance of the ritualism of the Old Testament.

As one examines the types and shadows of the Scriptures, one must be extremely careful not to read into the sacred text something that is not there. A person will do well if he takes as symbolic and typical only those things that are thus recognized by the inspired writers.

Untold damage has been done from time to time by overly zealous people in their attempts to see a typical or a symbolic meaning in certain persons or things in the Scriptures. The safest rule by which to be guided on this point may be stated thus: Recognize only those things as typical or symbolic which are thus designated in the Scriptures, and never give to any passage a typical meaning unless the Scriptures so indicate. To illustrate the point, let us look at an example or two. Joseph, we are often told, is a type of Christ. Isaac's taking Rebekah as his bride is also a type of Christ's taking His bride, the church. What inspired writer gives any indication to this effect? I have never seen anything in the Scriptures to warrant these positions. I admit that there are striking similarities in the cases; but analogies are not equivalent to a "thus saith the Lord." We do well, therefore, to have scriptural authority for whatever we say. One can, by allowing his imagination to run wild, see that a certain person or thing in the Old Testament is typical of something in the New. Another person, looking at the same thing, will see a different signification. Thus there are untold possibilities of speculation and error, which are dangerous whenever there is not a "thus saith the Lord" for a given position.

God has chosen certain things as symbols. For instance, beasts, as we learn from Daniel 7, are employed as emblems of world kingdoms. Whenever, therefore, a beast is thus used in the Scriptures and the facts of the context show that it has this metaphorical sense, one must understand that it signifies a civil government. God never mixes His symbols. Again, a pure, chaste virgin is used as a symbol of the true church. A harlot represents a false ecclesiasticism. God has interpreted these symbols. Man should not attach any signification to them other than that which was given by Him.

I might further illustrate this principle by calling attention to the Lord's Supper. The loaf represents the body of Jesus, whereas the fruit of the vine is symbolic of His blood. Whenever we see these emblems, we know their significance and do not attempt to read into them any idea other than that which the Lord Jesus gave them. Whenever we come to a symbol, we must therefore seek the divine interpretation of the same and never deviate from that meaning. **1st Corinthians 11: 24, 25**

FIGURATIVE LANGUAGE

The languages of all peoples seem to have begun largely with figures of speech — at least primitive writing indicates this position. It is by comparison that we appreciate and understand things. Thus figures have remained in our language and adorn it greatly. In fact, it is most difficult for us to speak without using some figures of speech. The Bible is no exception. One must therefore know the common figures of speech and how they are used in order to understand what the biblical writers meant.

The fact that a figurative expression occurs in a given passage is no warrant for one's taking its meaning and forcing it upon another passage, unless the facts of the given context show that the same figure was used in a like manner. To be more specific, let me call attention to the expression found in Ephesians regarding Christ's "having cleansed it [church] by the washing of water with the word" (**Eph. 5:26**). This statement is figurative language. We must not force this metaphorical sense upon another passage, which might in some way resemble this one passage, unless the facts of the latter context permit such an interpretation. **Romans 6 & St John 3**

Let us always bear in mind that figurative language, though elaborate and beautiful, stands for definite realities. It is therefore necessary for one to understand the figure and see the reality signified in order to comprehend the message wherever such usage is employed.

OBSCURE PASSAGES MUST BE INTERPRETED IN THE LIGHT OF PLAIN ONES

Whenever anyone sees that a passage is capable of more than one interpretation--viewed in the light of all the facts of the connection--he must select that translation or explanation which accords with plain statements found in other portions of the Word when rightly interpreted. As an illustration of this principle, I may call attention to **Hosea 3:1**, Then said the LORD unto me, Go yet, love a woman beloved of her friend, yet an adulteress, according to the love of the LORD toward the children of Israel, who look to other gods, and love flagons of wine. Without careful study of this text it would appear that God is telling Hosea to sin but we know this is not the case because **Romans 6:23** states that "the wages of sin is death" therefore we must do our due diligence to research the true meaning of the text.

What did the writer have in mind, when he, by the Spirit of God, used these words? One must study the entire text in order to see the proper connection; then he must compare all the facts discovered with statements found in other places which are capable of only one interpretation.

It is of utmost importance that one observes this rule. The assumption lying underneath it is that all truth harmonizes. Whenever there are any seeming discrepancies, the trouble lies with our non-comprehension of the data, or lack of the facts. 1st Corinthians 14:34

STUDYING THE EXACT GRAMMAR

In the English language there are eight parts of speech. These, taken together, constitute language. Each of them has a definite, specific use and relation to other parts of speech. It becomes absolutely necessary, if one is to arrive at the exact meaning of a word, that he know grammar, since each part of speech has a definite purpose and since words likewise have accurate definitions. One therefore must have an adequate knowledge of grammar and the meaning of words, if he is to arrive at the exact idea which the Holy Spirit had in mind.

By conservative scholars, the grammatical-historical principle of interpretation is the only one upon which a person can afford to rely. What is meant by this term? A person must acquire, if possible the historical data concerning any statement in order to see it in its proper perspective. He must, therefore, know the writer, the one to whom a document was sent, for what purpose it was written, and under what conditions in order to evaluate properly the message. He must also know the grammar thoroughly and the significance of language. With such definite information in hand, one can, by the aid of the Holy Spirit, understand the message. I, therefore, accept the correctness of this method of exegesis. Galatians 3:24-29 & Gen 3:16

THE MEANINGS OF WORDS

The student should have a good English dictionary at hand when he studies the Scriptures--unless he has an adequate idea of the vocabulary that is used in the Bible. If a person will only look in an unabridged dictionary of the English language, he will see that some words have many meanings or shades of ideas. This statement being true, one must know these various definitions in order to comprehend rightly the exact meaning of a given passage.

Though I am speaking simply from the English point of view, all Greek and Hebrew students know that the same principles apply with reference to the original text.

Whenever a word does have a number of meanings, we must select that one which will accord with all the facts of a given context, and which will not clash with any other plain statement of truth. i.e. fear: reverence

THE DIFFERENCE BETWEEN BIBLICAL AND PRESENT-DAY TERMINOLOGY

Our English dictionaries give the current meaning of words as they are employed now by the best speakers and writers. They also give colloquial usages. The Bible employs a certain definite usage that was current when the Scriptures were given. Sometimes, words have a meaning entirely different from what they had when our translation was made or when spoken originally. For instance, **a prophet** was simply a spokesman from God who delivered a message to the people. Sometimes he discussed things past; on other occasions, matters regarding things present in his day; and often those things lying in the future. At the present time, the word, "prophetic," as we have already noticed, is largely used with reference to future things. There are many changes that have taken place in our language. This fact demands that we compare scripture with scripture in order to see the usage to which a term was applied then. We must not therefore read back into the Scriptures definitions of words as they are being used today; because, as stated, practices have been introduced and changes have been made which have definitely determined present-day usage. We cannot therefore afford to read back into the Scriptures ideas and definitions of words as employed today unless we see from all the facts that the current meaning is in conformity with the biblical usage. **2nd Peter 1:3** A true prophet stays within the word of God.

Let Scripture Interpret Scripture.

A correct interpretation will always be consistent with the rest of the Scriptures. Therefore, it is essential for us as students of the Bible to interpret a passage in light of what the rest of the Scriptures say on the topic. There *are* Scriptures that are somewhat confusing. Peter himself tells us that (**2 Peter. 3:16-18**). When that is the case, rather than seeking to make an interpretation based on one verse, it is essential to examine other, perhaps more clear, passages of Scripture.

You recall there in the wilderness, Jesus was fasting for 40 days, when Satan came along to tempt him. We see there in that temptation something pretty interesting. Satan knows the Word of God. He seeks to lead Jesus astray from the will of His Father, by quoting **Psalm 91:11, 12**.

Satan said...

Matthew 4:6 "If You are the Son of God, throw Yourself down. For it is written: 'He shall give His angels charge over you,' and, 'In their hands they shall bear you up, Lest you dash your foot against a stone."

Satan left out an important phrase from that original text. He left out the phrase, "in all Your [God's] ways." According to the psalmist, a person is protected only when he is following the Lord's will. It was never intended for us to tempt God. But Jesus replied by interpreting Scripture with Scripture. What did He do? He quoted...

Deuteronomy 6:16 "You shall not tempt the LORD your God."

Jesus used Scripture to interpret Scripture when he was tempted by the devil. By doing this, Jesus was saying to us that a passage must be understood in the light of those clearer and more expressive scriptures.
So, if the section of scripture that you are seeking to interpret seems difficult, or vague, go to a clearer passage that speaks on the same subject, more thoroughly. This is important to do, or you can easily come to wrong conclusions.

Now, turn over with me to John chapter 10. With each of these rules that we'll look at, I'd like to show you how failing to follow the rule has led to a variety of wrong interpretations. Notice that in v.15 Jesus said, "As the Father knows Me, even so I know the Father; and I lay down My life for the *sheep*" (**John 10:15**). We might conclude, based on what Jesus says here, that the death He died on the cross was only for the sheep. And that is what some have concluded. There are Christians today who believe that Jesus' death on the cross only paid the price for a select group. They call this teaching "limited atonement." But we need to check Scripture with Scripture. When you do, what do you find out? You find out that Jesus died on the cross for everybody.

1 John 2:2 says...
"And He Himself is the propitiation for our sins, and not for ours only but also for the *whole* world."

1 Timothy 2:6 says that Jesus "gave Himself a ransom for all."

"Then," someone might ask, "why not are all people saved?"

Because the forgiveness of sins does not occur until a person turns from His sins to the Lord and places His trust in Jesus (**Acts 17:30**, **John 3:16**, **1 Jn. 5:12**). Christ's atonement is unlimited, but it's *application* is limited only to those who believe. If a person insists on opposing God and rejecting Him, then what Christ did on the cross for that person will not be applied to them. God will not force His salvation upon somebody who does not want it.

John 3:16 says...
"Whosoever *believes* in Him should not perish but have everlasting life."

Unbelief is the reason that some do not receive the benefits of Christ's death.

So, be careful not to base your conclusions, or build your interpretation of a Scripture on a single Scripture, but on Scripture as a whole. The Bible is the best interpreter of itself. Because that is the case, the first commentary you should consult on a passage is what the rest of the Scriptures have to say on the topic being examined. Commentaries, concordances, indexes in the back of your Bible and books on systematic theology can be very helpful in pointing out other verses on topics with which you may be unfamiliar. So, a rule or principle that we must follow: "Let Scripture interpret Scripture,"; this is incredibly simple and yet so important to put into practice!

The meaning of a word, phrase, sentence, or paragraph must be derived from the context.

The context of a passage is absolutely critical to properly interpreting the Bible. Why? Well…

- Every word _____.
- Every verse _____.
- Every paragraph _____.
- Every book _____.

Because that is the case, no verse of Scripture should be divorced from the verses around it. Interpreting a verse apart from its context is like trying to analyze:

– the President's speech by listening to a short sound bite
– a painting by looking at only a single square inch of the painting

Every word you interpret must be understood in the light of the words that come before and after it. Let me give you a couple of examples. Turn over to Colossians 3.

Colossians 3:15
"And let the peace of God rule in your hearts, to which also you were called in one body; and be thankful." NKJV

This verse is often quoted in studies about knowing the will of God. Why? Well, I've often heard that the word "rule" (v.15) in the Greek means "to arbitrate, or to govern." And that is correct. So, it has been said that we are to let the peace of God arbitrate or govern us as to our decisions. How do we know the will of God? Some say:

– Having peace about something indicates God's "green light."
– Lacking peace about something indicates God's "red light."

But, hold on a second, is that what that verse is talking about? Not at all. Let's read the verse in its context. Let's start back in v.12.

Colossians 3:12-16

12 Therefore, as the elect of God, holy and beloved, put on tender mercies, kindness, humility, meekness, longsuffering; **13** bearing with one another, and forgiving one another, if anyone has a complaint against another; even as Christ forgave you, so you also must do. **14** But above all these things put on love, which is the bond of perfection. **15** And let the peace of God rule in your hearts, to which also you were called in one body; and be thankful." (NKJV)

Paul's not talking about *decision making* or discerning the will of God at all! Paul is instructing them about *unity* in the body!

Notice, he talks about…

"bearing with one another" (v.13)
"forgiving one another" (v.13)

"put on love, which is the bond of perfection" (v.14)

We are to as Christians "let the peace of God rule [our] hearts." That's what Paul is saying. It is wrong to take this verse out of context and use it as a proof text to support the teaching that: "Having a peace about something confirms whether or not something is God's will for your life."

Let me ask you a question...
When God told Moses that His will for Moses' life, was to go back to Pharaoh and tell him to let my people go, do you think Moses had a peace about it? (**Exodus chapter 3 thru 12**) no, he was full of fear and doubt.

Did that mean that that wasn't God's will for his life? No.

How about Gideon? Did he have peace as he heard God's will for his life? No, he was very fearful.

How about the disciples out there on the storm tossed Sea of Galilee? Did they have a peace about it? If anybody could be sure that they were in the center of God's will, it was those men! Jesus told them to go right out into the storm!!

As Christians we *are* to have the peace of God that surpasses understanding (**Phil 4:7**) but a lack of peace does not confirm that something is not God's will. A lack of peace may be because of unbelief, lack of faith, or our unwillingness to trust the Lord.

Isaiah 26:3 says..
"You will keep him in perfect peace, whose mind is stayed on

thee, because he trusts in thee." KJV

A lack of peace may simply indicate that a person needs to trust God, or go to Him again in prayer. If Christians only moved out in faith when they had peace about things, I imagine there would be far less ventures of faith taking place, far less witnessing.

Another example of a verse that is often lifted out of context would be **Isaiah 53:5**. There you are praying for a person, and one of the other persons who prays says something like, "Lord we know that you are going to heal this person because Your Word says…

Isaiah 53:5c
"…And with his stripes we are healed." KJV
Have you heard that verse used in such a way? I have. Well, if you examine Isaiah 53 you'll notice that it doesn't have anything to do with physical healing. The passage is about what the Messiah's death would do for our spiritual condition, and the healing of our sins, not our physical bodies.

So again, to rightly interpret God's Word you have to be very careful to consider the context of the passage, i.e., that which has just been said and that which follows.

Interpret the Scriptures knowing that the goal in interpretation is not to discover hidden, secret truths, or to be unique in your interpretation.

God has given us His Word in order to reveal Himself.

- It is not a book of dark mysteries, and riddles, it is a book of

self-disclosure.
– He is not a God of confusion, but of clarity.
– He has not spoken in order to conceal, but to be understood and known.

Therefore, when we come to His Word we need to realize that it is the plain meaning of the text that we are seeking to understand.

We need not look for hidden or cryptic truths. God has preserved His Word to speak to the multitudes of ordinary people that they might be saved. So, don't pass up the obvious and natural meaning of a text looking for something "unique" and "deep."

Many of the times someone has excitedly shared with me something really "unique" and "deep" that they discovered in the Bible, something they've never heard any teacher share, they have usually been wrong. It is tempting as you study the Scriptures to discover things that no one else has ever seen before. But if you're discovering things like that, you can almost bet that you are making the Scriptures to say things that were never intended by the original authors.

Unique interpretations are usually wrong.

This is not to say that the correct understanding of a text may not often seem unique to someone who hears it for the first time. But it is to say that unique interpretation should not be your aim.

Your goal is to discover the plain, simple, straight forward meaning of the text, the meaning the original author intended to communicate.

Interpret the Scriptures, literally, unless you have good reason to believe that they are figurative.

There are those today, and there have been those throughout Church history that have believed that Scripture has hidden, secret, mystical meanings underneath the plain and obvious meaning of a text. That is, they believe that although the Scriptures say one thing, they actually signify something else, something other than what is said. Some of the early church fathers (men like Clement of Alexandria, Origen, Augustine, and Jerome) believed that every Scripture had two, three, even four or five interpretations.

Their influence led to the widespread medieval belief that every verse of Scripture had numerous meanings.

Many of the early church fathers were influenced in this direction by the Greek philosophers who did this with the writings of Homer and Hesiod. This method (or approach) to interpreting the Bible is called the: "Allegorical method" To allegorize is to say, "Well, in this passage, this represents this, and this represents that, and basically, this whole story is a picture of this..." That is to turn a passage of Scripture into a spiritual parable, some story with a deeper meaning.

There are hundreds of examples by well-known teachers through church history who have done this!

Here are some examples: Do you recall the story of Jacob and his two wives in **Genesis 29**? Well, one teacher said that Leah represents the Jews, Rachel represents the church, and Jacob represents Jesus who serves both. Another has said that as Aaron and Hur held up Moses' hands, it was an Old Testament picture of

Christ on the cross. One said that the twelve stones taken from the Jordan River represent the 12 apostles. One said that the field in the book of Ruth is really a reference to the Bible. Ruth represents students. The reapers in the field represent teachers. One said that the Red Sea symbolizes the atoning blood of Christ. One said that five kings who attacked Gibeon in Joshua chapter 10 represent the five senses: sight, hearing, taste, touch, and smell.

Why is allegorizing and spiritualizing the Scriptures dangerous?

A. Allegorized interpretations are not based on anything objective. They can't be verified. They are based solely on the subjective preferences and whims of the interpreter's imagination. This becomes obvious when you hear another person teach on the same passage and they have an entirely different twist on the story. One person says that such and such a thing represents this, while another person says it really represents this. This is one of the reasons allegorized interpretations are dangerous.

There are no guidelines, or boundaries.

B. A spiritualization of the Scriptures doesn't have any authority. I've heard some teachers say some things and I've wanted to stand up and say, "How do you know that? Show us how you've come to your conclusions. Show me in the Word." If it can't be shown in the Word of God, then the words of the preacher lose their authority.

This allegorical method of interpretation that led to these kinds of interpretations, dominated most of Christian history. It was not until the time of the Reformation during the 1500 - 1600s that there was a major turning away from this approach to interpreting the Bible. Men like John Wycliffe, Martin Luther, John Calvin, William Tyndale, and John Knox saw the dangers and the problems with this method and took a stand for a literal method of Bible interpretation.

John Calvin said that allegorical interpretations were "frivolous games" and that to interpret the word in that way was to torture the Scriptures.

Martin Luther strongly denounced this method...

He said: "When I was a monk, I was an expert in allegories. I allegorized everything.....I consider the ascription of several senses to Scripture to be not merely dangerous and useless for teaching but even to cancel the authority of Scripture whose meaning ought to be always one and the same....Allegories are empty speculations and as it were the scum of Holy Scripture."

Martin Luther became a strong advocate instead for a literal method.

...a method in which, the only meaning which one may ascribe to the text is that which the author intended, as one is able to reconstruct it in the historical context and with ordinary rules of grammar.

These men's rejection of the allegorical approach to Scripture was revolutionary. And it was with them, that the allegorical stronghold on the church began to crumble. And from that point forward much of the church has gone back to interpreting the Word of God literally.

Now, why do we believe that interpreting the Word of God literally is actually the way God desires that we interpret it?

There are a couple of reasons. The best reason though is because Jesus consistently interpreted the Word of God literally. Whether it was the Old Testament account of...

The Creation account of Adam and Eve

_____

Noah's Ark and the flood

_____

Jonah and the great fish

_____

Sodom and Gomorrah

_____

Or the account of Lot and his wife

_____

Jesus (and the New Testament authors) consistently interpreted these stories literally as actual historical events. So, if Jesus and the New Testament authors interpreted the Bible literally, then we must also. There were no esoteric, mystical, allegorical, or spiritualized interpretations!!!

Now, when we talk about the need to interpret the Scriptures literally, that does not mean we are ignorant of the use of certain grammatical devices (similes, personification, metaphors, symbolic language)

1 Peter 5:8 says...
Your adversary, the devil, prowls about like a roaring lion, seeking someone to devour."

It's clear that Peter is using a figure of speech. He's comparing the devil to a lion. It does tell us something very literally about the nature and purpose of the devil. It is easy to understand that when Jesus said that He was "the vine" and the disciples were "the branches" that He was speaking figuratively.

There are times when it is less obvious that the author is speaking metaphorically or figuratively. But there are usually some clues that are built into the context. We'll talk about those clues in an upcoming class. So don't read into the text things that were not intended by the original author. Let the text speak for itself rather than reading into the text things that aren't there. When you approach the Scriptures, keep in mind that what a passage means was fixed by the author and is not subject to alteration. Your goal is to: discover the author's intended meaning, the only true meaning. A text cannot mean what it never meant. Meaning is determined by an author; it is discovered by the reader.

It is common for Bible study leaders in small groups to go around the circle after reading a passage of Scripture and ask the people:

"What does this verse mean to you Steve?"

Steve says, "To me, this verse means…"

And the leader will say, "Oh that's interesting. I haven't heard that before."

"What does this verse mean to you Lisa?"

Lisa will say, "To me, this verse means something entirely different…"

And she goes on to give an entirely different interpretation.

"Interesting."

"Wow that really blesses me."

Well, the question that the leader asked, "What does this mean to you?" is not a question that really matters.

The question that matters is: "What does this verse mean?" **PERIOD.**

A **better question** for the study leader to ask would be:

"How does this verse *apply* to you."

There are many different ways of applying a Scripture, but there is still only one correct meaning for each passage.

That is the author's intended meaning. *That* is the meaning that we are after.

Biblical Interpretation

The word *interpret* can be used to mean "to understand," "to translate," or "to explain." These three functions of the interpretive process are also appropriate for preaching. First we seek to understand *what the text is saying*. Then we translate that information into the *intended theological message*. Finally, we explain *that message to the congregation*.

The interpreter needs to have a working knowledge of basic principles of interpretation. These hermeneutical principles are like the tricks of the trade for an interpreter. They guide us in our examination of the text so that our work is kept within the bounds of legitimate hermeneutics. The assumption behind these principles is that, properly handled, the text will disclose its meaning to the interpreter. Interpreting the Bible—**hermeneutics**—is the science and art of understanding, translating, and explaining the meaning of the scripture text. To guide this process, the preacher can follow basic principles that help the interpreter discern the intended meaning of the text's writer rather than imposing his own ideas on the text. Here are seven principles I would recommend.

What is the essence of the text?

Bible scholars call this the *genre* of the text. That means the general form the text takes—narrative, prophecy, poetry, history, gospel, and epistle. The various kinds of literature present their message in differing styles and with different structure. Narrative texts (an account of events) do not operate the same way epistles (letter of instructions) do in getting their message across to the reader.

Consider the context of the passage for a better understanding of its meaning.

This is often considered the first and most important principle for accurate interpretation. Bible scholars use the term *context* to discuss various aspects of the original writing of the text—historical, social, political, religious, and literary. It is this literary concern I have in mind as the *context* of the passage.

The writer follows a logical line of thought in what he writes. What he said in the previous verses or chapters and what he said in the ones that follow will help make the text in question clear. Taking the text out of that context risks misinterpreting it. Often clues in the surrounding verses will open aspects of the meaning in your text you would have otherwise missed.

Read the text for its plain and obvious meaning.

A common and persistent myth about the Bible is that its real meaning is hidden behind the surface message. Even though the Bible uses symbolic or figurative language, most of it is clear to the reader. Even when you do not know about the people, places, and events in question, you can grasp the point of the text.

The use of figurative language in Scripture only enhances the plain meaning of the text. "Why do you complain about the splinter in your brother's eye when you have a plank in your own eye?" Jesus said (Matt. 7:3 NIV). Even though this is figurative language, we have no trouble understanding what he meant. His use of the metaphors makes it even clearer.

Try to discern the writer's intentions when he wrote the text.

This principle of intentionality is critical for the expository preacher. You study the text not to find a sermon in it but to discover the writer's intended message. Unless you can learn the intended meaning of the text writer, you will not be able to preach the message of the text in your sermon. Remember, "The text cannot mean what it never meant." Discovering the writer's original meaning is your first task as you prepare to preach to your own generation.

The intended meaning of the text writer will also be the intended meaning of the Holy Spirit who inspired him to write. As you read his words, you are dealing with a revelation from God. Remember, "All scripture is given by the inspiration of God" (**2 Tim. 3:16** KJV). The same Holy Spirit who inspired these words in the first place wants this message to be preached again through your sermon.

And you want to preach in a way that is in line with the Spirit's purposes.

Look carefully at the language of the text for what it reveals about its meaning.

Words carry thoughts. The words of the text are all we have of the writer's thoughts. If he hadn't written it down, we wouldn't know what he was thinking. So we can look closely at his words, examining each one carefully for the part it plays in his message. Also look at how the words and phrases connect with one another and how the sentences are constructed.

If you can study the text in the original language, you can gain greater insight into the meaning. Many preachers study Greek and Hebrew for that reason. But even if you cannot read your texts in those languages, you can still use lexicons and word study books to guide you. Though your congregation is probably not interested in the Hebrew and Greek, your study will open insights that will make the message clearer to them. You can do this without going into detail about tenses and forms in the original languages.

Notice the various theological themes in the text.

Though a text has one intended meaning, it can have a number of significant theological themes. It can also have a number of different applications. When you do the structural diagram and your observations, you will list these themes and what the text says about them. Identifying these themes and understanding how they relate to one another in your text is a most helpful key to grasping its meaning.

These same theological themes will show up in different combinations in various texts throughout the Bible. In your preaching text, you will try to discover the best wording for the writer's *subject* and the *modifier* that limits and focuses it. You will also look through the text for the *predicates,* the various things the writer is saying about his subject. The theological themes in the text will give you what you need for these tasks.

Always take a God-centered perspective for interpreting your text.

This means looking at the text in terms of what it reveals about God and his dealings with his creation, particularly man. This is theological interpretation. It arises from the assumption that the Bible is really God's means of making himself known to us. What it says about him will always be central to every text. The Bible was not given by God to tell us about ancient religious people and how we should all try to be like them. It was given to tell us about the faithful God whom they either served or denied. Their response is not the central message; God's will and his involvement with his creation are. Even texts that give instructions as to how we should behave reveal something about God.

Notes

CHAPTER FIVE

S.O.A.P.
SCRIPTURE, OBSERVATION, APPLICATION, PRAYER

S.O.A.P- Scripture, Observation, Application, Prayer.

Three things you will need to complete your sermon

1. _____
2. _____
3. _____

What is Homiletics?

Homiletics is derived from the word homily, which means a sermon or to preach. Thus homiletics is concerned with the art of preaching. How do we write and prepare sermons?

Studying homiletics helps to improve your skill at communicating the gospel and other biblical topics. You don't have to be a Bible scholar, a theologian or leader. It is a tool to help you analyze a passage of scripture to more fully understand what God is saying to His people.

Pray, read, meditate, introduction, main points, supporting points, rhetoric, analogy etc.

What is Hermeneutics?

Hermeneutics is the art of interpreting text. This has been used by philosophers etc. It is not just the interpretation of the Bible, but includes the general interpretation of text.

_____
_____
_____

Why is Hermeneutics an important subject and why study it?

What it meant is what it means. Meaning is not something we get to read into the text on the basis of our own opinions or ideas. Meaning is something that resides in the text, having being placed there by the inspired author; and requires of us to discover what that meaning is by proper contextual study of the text.

Significance however is a different matter altogether. A text can have significance or even application for you or me, which the original author could never have imagined. But the text cannot have a meaning that the original inspired author did not place there. Meaning is one thing, significance or application, another.

Context is king

Words only have meaning in context. Plucking words out of contexts and linking them to other uses of the same word is often the recipe for disaster and misinterpretation.

The difference between meaning and application is vitally important! Often, we mistake the two. The Bible essentially offers one meaning, but the applications, significance etc. are countless!

Why is context important?

1. **Literal Meaning-** _____
   _____

2. **Historical Setting-** _____
   _____

3. **Grammar-** _____
   _____

4. **Synthesis** _____
   _____

Context avoids Error

• Taking phrases and verses out of context always leads to misunderstanding. For instance, taking the phrase "God is love" (**1 John 4:7-16**) out of its context, we might come away thinking that our God loves everything and everyone at all times with a gushing, romantic love. But in its literal and grammatical context, "love" here refers to agape love, the essence of which is sacrifice for the benefit of another, not a sentimental, romantic love.

• The historical context is also crucial, because John was addressing believers in the first century church and instructing them not on God's love per se, but on how to identify true believers from false professors. True love— the sacrificial, beneficial kind—is the mark of the true believer (v. 7), those who do not love do not belong to God (v. 8), God loved us before we loved Him (vv. 9-10), and all of this is why we should love one another and thereby prove that we are His (v. 11-12)

EXEGESIS AND EISEGESIS

- Exegesis is not hermeneutics

- Hermeneutics is the field of study concerned with how we interpret the Bible. Exegesis is the actual interpretation of the Bible by drawing the meaning out of the Biblical text.

- Exegesis is the explanation of a text based on a careful, objective analysis, it literally means **"to lead out of."** That means that the interpreter is led to his conclusions by following the text.

- **Eisegesis is the interpretation of a passage based on a subjective, non-analytical reading.** The word Eisegesis literally means **"to lead into,"** which means the interpreter injects his own ideas into the text, making it mean whatever he wants.

- **Eisegesis** is a mishandling of the text and often leads to a misinterpretation. **Exegesis** is concerned with discovering the true meaning of the text, respecting its grammar, syntax, and setting. **Eisegesis** is concerned only with making a point, even at the expense of the meaning of words.

Exegesis

- 1) **Observation:**
  _____

- 2) **Interpretation:**
  _____

- 3) **Correlation:**
  _____

- 4) **Application:**
  _____

Eisegesis

- 1) **Imagination:**
  _____

- 2) **Exploration:**
  _____

- 3) **Application:**
  _____

"Again I tell you, it is easier for a camel to go through the eye of a needle than for someone who is rich to enter the kingdom of God."

Matthew 19:24

- Exegesis vs Eisegesis? – What would you say?   What is the meaning of this text?

Notes

CHAPTER SIX

THE PREACHER EXEGESIS WORKSHEET

The Preacher's Exegesis Work Sheet

Opening:

Before the preacher/teacher begins to study the word of God, they must be in a prayerful state of mind. In essence, one must leave the modern world to enter the world of the Bible. A quiet place is necessary to hear God's still voice. One must prepare to study. As an athlete warms up by stretching their muscles, the preacher/interpreter must spiritually "warm" up to enter the presence of God

Sounding:

The passage under study has a context. Listen with the imagination to hear the sounds in the text. It demands that one make uses of the five senses to go there. Reading the passage several times can aid this process. One may record themselves reading the passage to capture nuances. Keep in mind that the scriptures were spoken before they were written.

Savoring:

Look for images and ideas that spring from the text. Past readings will inform your ability to use your creative imagination. Use your powers of observation to see what you may have missed before. The Holy Spirit will bring to your memory past truth that you have experienced.

Word Study:

Working knowledge of the original languages is helpful in doing word study. However, if you had not had the opportunity to study them, there are many helps on the market that will assist you.

Commentary
Biblical tools
History
Geography
Maps

The Preacher's Exegesis Work Sheet

Shaping:

What shape is the message beginning to take? By this time in the preparation process you begin to see the direction the text is taking you, by the Holy Spirit's leading.

1. What event comes to mind?
2. What person/people come to mind?

3. What other scriptures come to mind?
4. As you visualize the group you will be speaking to what feeling or thoughts or questions enter your consciousness?

The sermon purpose statement

Situation: what are you aiming to accomplish through this message/lesson?

Example: I want to encourage the congregation to have more of an attitude of gratitude.

Goal: I want to lead the people to experience the joy of living a thanksgiving life

Topics

The Preacher's Exegesis Work Sheet

The Text

A) Who's Present?

_____
_____
_____
_____

B) What's the occasion?

_____
_____
_____
_____

C) What's the setting? Formal? Informal?

_____
_____
_____
_____

D) What does the text call for the hearer? Preacher? God?

_____
_____
_____
_____

The Preacher's Exegesis Work Sheet

E) Is anyone changed? Why or Why Not?

_____
_____
_____
_____

F) What is the setting? The Temperature? Emotional level?

_____
_____
_____
_____

G) How does the text read from the inside, the other side?

_____
_____
_____
_____

H) What does the author of the text tell us about himself, past, present, and future?

_____
_____
_____
_____

The Preacher's Exegesis Work Sheet

ANALYSIS

SUBJECTS

_____
_____
_____
_____

SITUATION

_____
_____
_____
_____

STRUCTURE

_____
_____
_____
_____

SUBJECT TESTIMONY/RESPONSE

_____
_____
_____
_____

SCRIPTURE TEACHING/TRUTH

_____
_____
_____
_____

The Preacher's Exegesis Work Sheet

SERMON SHAPE

(1) PROSPECTIVE
   Right-handed (images)

_____
_____

_____
_____

    Left-handed (ideals)

_____
_____
_____
_____

    (2) PROPORTION

Gospel_____
_____
_____
_____

Law

_____
_____
_____
_____

The Preacher's Exegesis Work Sheet

_____
_____
_____
_____

(3) PROGRESSION

    Then – Biblical Context

_____
_____
_____
_____

    Now – Contemporary Situation

_____
_____
_____
_____

The Preacher's Exegesis Work Sheet

APPLICATION

A) Have you come to terms with the truth of the text?

_____
_____
_____
_____

B) What is the truth for the Preacher?

_____
_____
_____
_____

C) What is the truth for the People?

_____
_____
_____
_____

D) Is it evangelistic?

_____
_____
_____
_____

E) Is it practical?

_____
_____
_____
_____

F) Is it Eternal?

_____
_____
_____
_____

The Preacher's Exegesis Work Sheet

G) What is the application for:

Senior Citizens

_____
_____

Youth

_____
_____

Children

_____
_____

Singles

_____
_____

Young Adults

_____

_____

ILLUSTRATIONS

1. Family
2. Business
3. Animals
4. Athletics
5. Common objects
6. Current events
7. Nature
8. Friendships
9. Education
10. Travel
11. Music
12. Politics
13. Internet
14. The Preacher's Exegesis

15) Other preachers

What are the power points for the Preacher/Interpreter in the passage?

1. _____
   _____
2. _____
   _____

3. _____

4. _____

5. _____

What are the power points for the people in the passage?

6. _____

7. _____

8. _____

9. _____

10. _____

The Preacher's Exegesis Work Sheet

THE CELEBRATION WORKSHEET

A. Does the text celebrate?
B. What does it celebrate?
C. What material of celebration can we use? (Song/poem/life/experience/current/event/personal/etc.)

QUESTIONS TO CONSIDER:

1) What voice will best suit this sermon?
   a.) Empathy
   b.) Sympathy
   c.) Commanding
   d.) Exhorting

2) How will the sermon sound to those hearing it in the pew?
   a.) Convicting
   b.) Confronting
   c.) Challenging
   d.) Encouraging
3) Is the sermon Christ centered?

Celebration: How will you celebrate or reinforce the truth of the message?

_____
_____
_____
_____
_____
_____
_____

CHAPTER SEVEN
EVANGELISM

*The fruit of the righteous is a tree of life; and he that **winneth** souls is wise. Proverbs 11:30*

Evangelism:

1. the practice of spreading the Christian gospel
2. passionate or intense missionary zeal for the cause
3. the work, methods, or characteristic outlook of a revivalist or evangelist preacher

True Evangelism

Evangelism is not based on religion, denomination, race, creed or color and is not subject to the tradition of men, however, it is a ministry that has been given by God to the born-again believer.
2 Corinthians 5:17, 18 *"therefore if any man be in Christ, he is a new creature: old things are past away; behold, all things are become new. And all things are of God, who hath reconciled us to himself by Jesus Christ, and hath given to us the ministry of reconciliation;"* Therefore we must seek understanding of God's purpose for evangelizing. True evangelism should be in the heart of each leader who is called by God, especially seeing that God has giving us the great commission of *Luke 14:23* "And the lord said unto the servant, Go out into the highways and hedges, and **compel** them to come in, that my house may be filled."

We should take our examples of evangelism from the Bible (for example Mark 6: 7-13) here we read where Jesus calls the twelve that he has chosen. Then he sends them out, but not without transferring of power and instructions. That's why it is important to have on your evangelizing team one that is filled with the spirit of the living God. As a leader in your church, you should be able to identify who has a heart for evangelism. ,

The instructions given should be followed, so that we can achieve maximum outcome. "Take nothing for their journey save a staff only; no scrip, no bread, no money in their purse:" These where the instructions for the disciples. We must use wisdom and be led by the spirit because of the different times and demographics we now live in. "Scrip" means a small piece of paper with writing on it. I do want to point out one thing. We have to be careful not to sound like telemarketers with a pre-written script for every person.. Each person is different, therefore we must be led by the spirit as to what should be said.

As we continue to look at true evangelism through the eyes of Mark we find that we must prepare ourselves for rejection as well as acceptance. The instructions are, if you are not received or they don't what to hear you, knock the dust off your feet. In other words, keep it moving. Before we can see the effects of evangelism in our churches we must first "Go!" The Bible says that "they went out and preached that men should repent and they casted out many devils and anointed with oil many that were sick and healed them." As an evangelist, the kingdom agenda should be our focus at all times.

Our hope is that our churches are full, but our call is to reconcile the lost back to God, heal the sick and cast out devils whether they step foot into our churches or not.

The Who?

There is a misconception in the church world that says we should evangelize the poor, the hungry and the homeless only. On the contrary, Jesus evangelized both the 'haves' and the 'have nots'. We must not limit our evangelism reach to the tradition of our denominations. Luke paints a beautiful picture of just who we should evangelize. **Luke 5:1-7** *1 And it came to pass, that, as the people pressed upon him to hear the word of God, he stood by the lake of Gennesaret, ² And saw two ships standing by the lake: but the fishermen were gone out of them, and were washing their nets. ³ And he entered one of the ships, which was Simon's, and prayed him that he would thrust out a little from the land. And he sat down, and taught the people out of the ship. ⁴ Now when he had left speaking, he said unto Simon, launch out into the deep, and let down your nets for a draught. ⁵ And Simon answering said unto him, Master, we have toiled all the night, and have taken nothing: nevertheless, at thy word I will let down the net. ⁶ And when they had this done, they enclosed a great multitude of fishes: and their net brake. ⁷ And they beckoned unto their partners, which were in the other ship, that they should come and help them. And they came, and filled both the ships, so that they began to sink.*

When we read the writings of Luke, we see that Jesus is evangelizing the working class, we never know what a person can possibly bring to the table ie: gifts and talents. **Verse 10 & 11** show us that the natural ability that one possesses can be cultivated and used for the kingdom of God. These men had just been evangelized and are headed to their new profession (fishers of men). We see in the text that it didn't make Jesus any difference when it came to their economic status. We also must approach our evangelism with this same mind set and be led by the spirit of God.

Beyond the four walls

In order for us to be effective in evangelism we must be willing to go outside of the four walls of our church. In **Luke 14:23** we find Jesus instructing believers to go out and compel people to come, the apostle Paul is a good example of one who evangelizes outside of the church as you read throughout the book of **Acts.** It is a necessity for us to go out and evangelize, if we are to have growth in the kingdom of God. Before we look at ***Luke 6:17,*** Jesus calls the first disciples and heals all manner of sickness in **Luke 5.** Now in Luke 6 he begins to teach in the synagogue aka the church. If we are not careful, we will become at ease in Zion and stay within the walls of the church, but Jesus leads them out of the synagogue where he reaches the masses and begins to minister. The Bible says in **2 Corinthians 4:3** "But if our gospel be hid it is hid to them that are lost". It is our responsibility as ministers of reconciliation to evangelize the lost back unto God, being mindful that we are not trying to build a kingdom unto ourselves, for Jesus says in **Luke 4:43** I must preach the kingdom of God to other cities also: for therefore am I sent.

Rest

It is important that we make time to rest. We have a tendency to go and go and go without resting or checking in with God to see if we are still in alignment with the assignment. Let's look at the greatest evangelist to walk this earth, in **Mark 4:35-39. W**e see where Jesus is asleep in the bottom of the ship and this was shortly after he had evangelized the twelve disciples. Here he leads by example and rests. In **Mark 6:30, 31,** he instructs the apostles to withdraw themselves from the people and rest. Jesus understands the importance of rest and made time to do just that. We as born again believers must follow suit. When we rest we are rejuvenated and our minds are clear to hear our next instructions. We read in **Genesis 2:1-3** that God rested after completing His creation. God gives us an opportunity to rest in him according to **Hebrews 4.** When we rest in him, we cease from doing our own works and totally rely on God,. So when we evangelize, it's not us but the Christ in us; because we understand as believers that true evangelism can only be achieved when we rest in Him.

Notes

ABOUT THE AUTHOR

Pastor Byron Holloway was baptized and filled with the gift of the Holy Ghost in 1994 at Gloryland Apostolic Cathedral in Richmond California under the leadership of Bishop Tom H. Watson. He was appointed deacon fulfilling all of the duties according to the word of God. (*I Timothy 3:8*) During that time, he also served as Sunday School Superintendent, Adult Sunday School Teacher, and a member on the Board of Trustees. Pastor Holloway accepted his call to preach and teach the Gospel of Jesus Christ on June 17, 1997. He was appointed Youth Pastor and began to build the youth ministry with fellowships in cities like Oakland, Fresno, Atwater, Pittsburg, and Los Angeles.

In March of 2003 God led Pastor Holloway to The Lord's House of Worship under the leadership of Pastor Greg D. Williams where he was ordained Elder. Once again, he was appointed the Sunday School Superintendent and Youth Leader, teaching the young people how to live for Christ.

God spoke to Pastor Holloway concerning a new ministry in January of 2006. After much fasting and praying Living Bread Ministries was birthed in the city of Vallejo Ca. and **"To God be the Glory!"**

During the ministries last eleven years, Souls have been added to the Kingdom and Miracles of Healing are evident by the power of the Holy Ghost. Pastor Byron Holloway has devoted himself to studying and researching the word of God.

Pastor Holloway is married to Evangelist Gwendolyn Holloway and together they have five children. Jocelyn, Bryan, Nicholas, Jazmyn, and Daniel.

www.ingramcontent.com/pod-product-compliance
Lightning Source LLC
Chambersburg PA
CBHW072202100426
42738CB00011BA/2545